Beer

Vintage Pictures and advertising

Retro Books

Presentation

This book consists of a non-systematic series of images to collect, see, and, above all, to use for decoration purposes.

It was designed so that you can detach all images or each one individually, allowing you to frame the pictures you like the most.

The purpose of this book is aesthetic only, to assemble together beautiful images which take us to charming places in the history of great brands of food and drinking products. It is a tribute to so many advertisement creators and label designers that will forever remain in our memories.

For this reason, we do not indicate dates or researches that we made throughout the process of making this book.

Retro Books

THE HOSTESS.

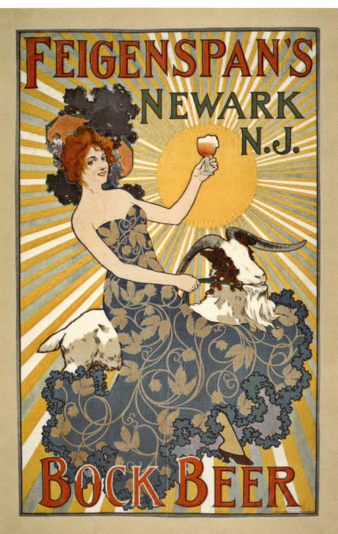

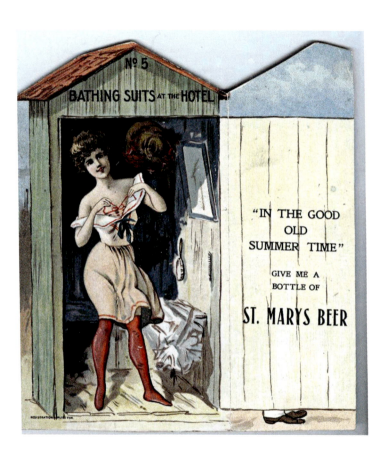

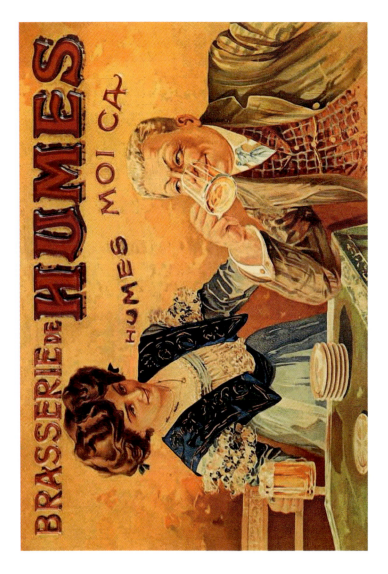

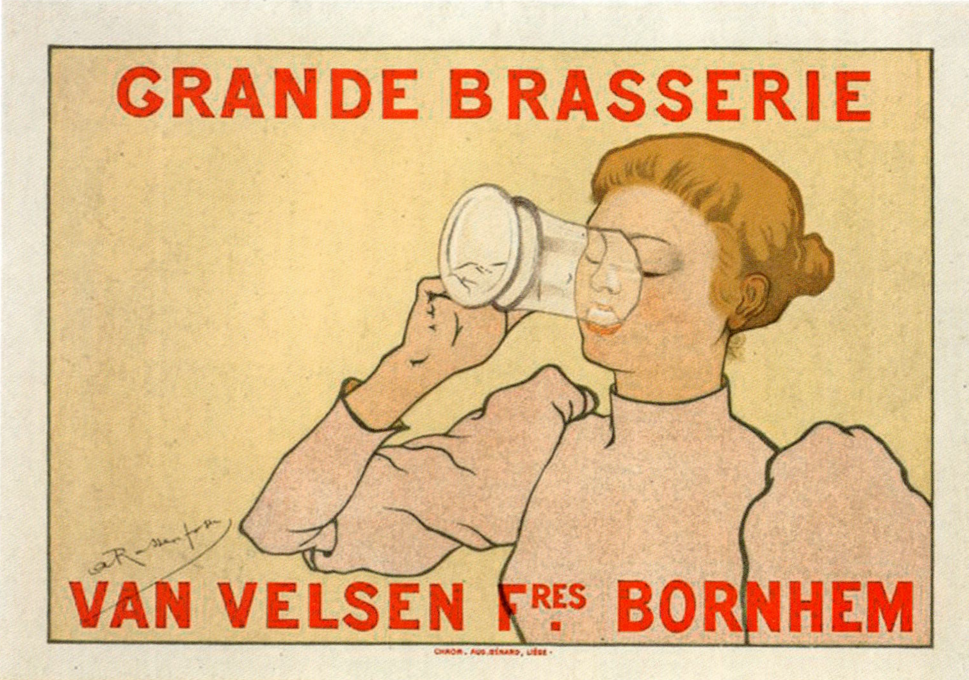
GRANDE BRASSERIE
VAN VELSEN F.RES BORNHEM
CHROM. AUG. BÉNARD, LIÈGE.

LAGER BEER

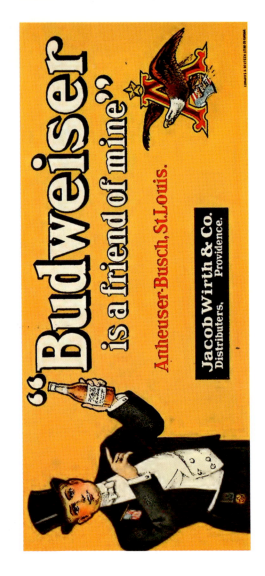

H. CLAUSEN & SON
BOCK BEER
HOPS
A.N.J.
HOPS
A.N.J.
G. MALT Co
G. MALT Co
G. MALT Co
G. MALT Co
BREWERY,
47TH ST. & 2ND AV.
1879
NEW YORK.
G.W. & C.R. MILLER
BOSTON.
SOLE AGENTS.

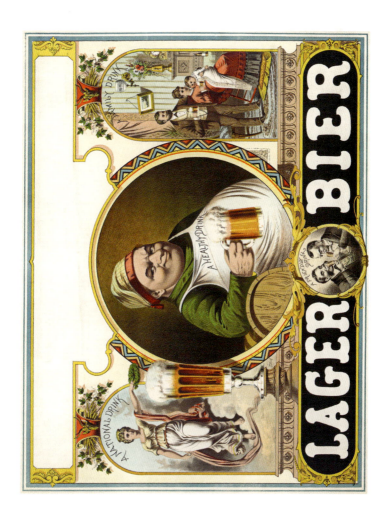

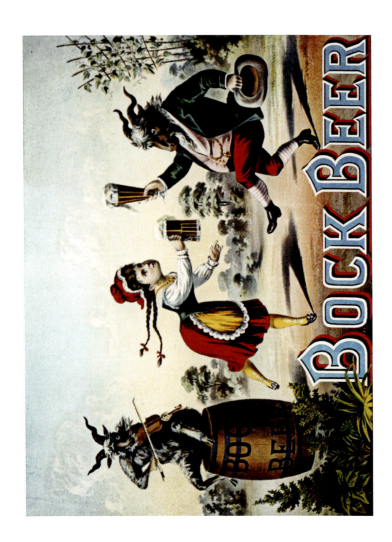

Well Earned Supremacy
John L. Sullivan
Super Champion
"Well Earned Supremacy"
Hohenadel
BEER

Geo. Winter Brewing Co.

Bock Beer

BREWERY. 55th St. Betw. 2d & 3d Avs. N.Y.

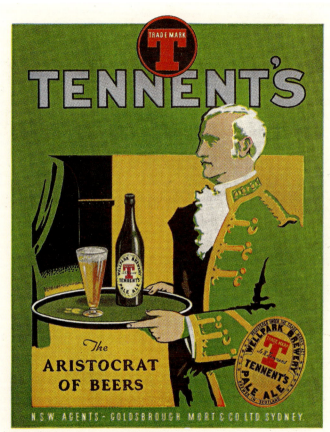

INCORPORATED IN VICTORIA

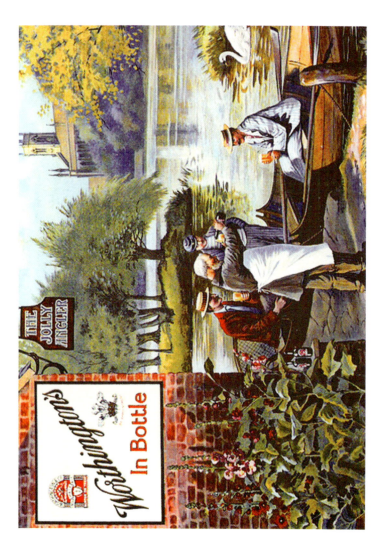

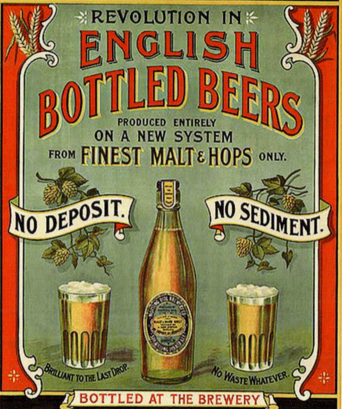

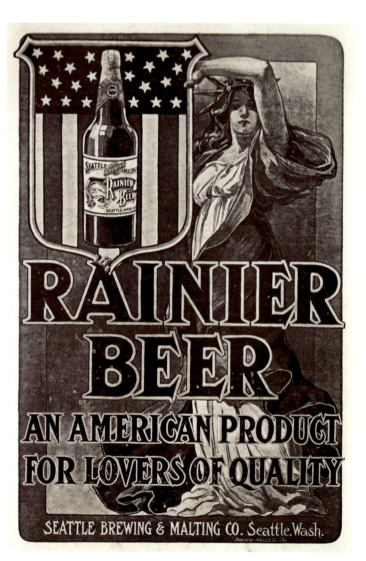

FRESH AND COLD
LAGER BEER
DIRECT FROM THE
NORTH POLE.
LITH. BY A. HOEN & CO. BALTIMORE, MD.
PUBLISHED BY F. KLEMM, No. 254 N. CENTRAL AVE., BALTIMORE.

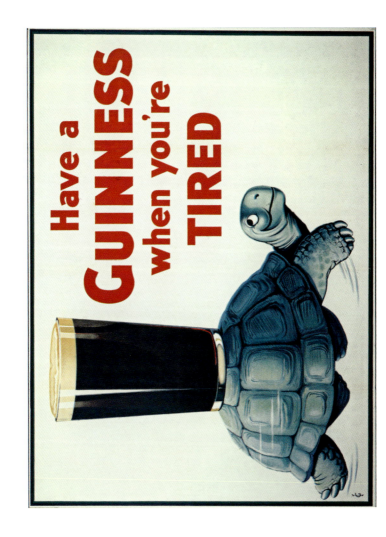

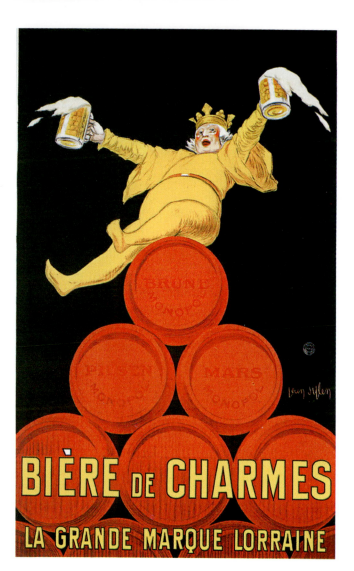

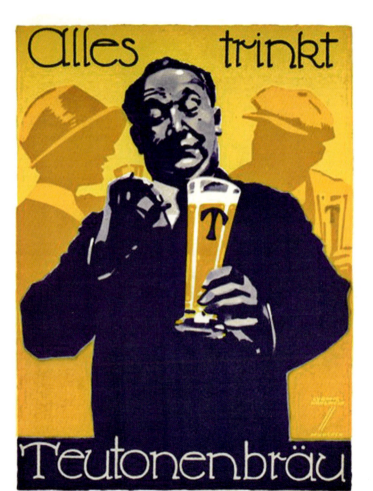

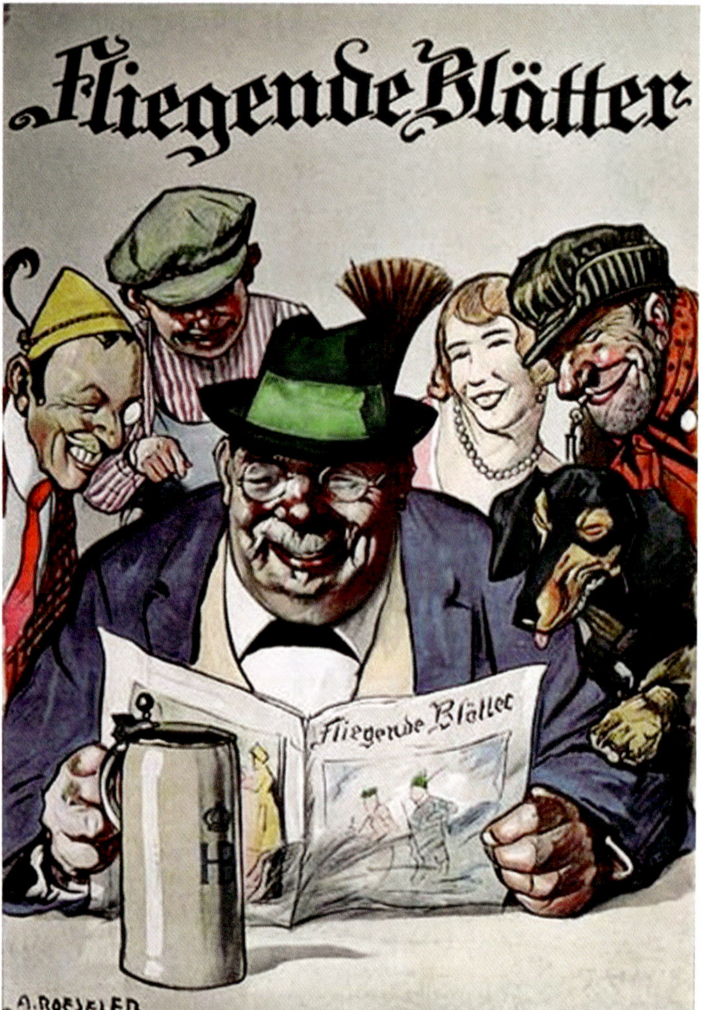

Fliegende Blätter
Fliegende Blätter
A. ROESELER

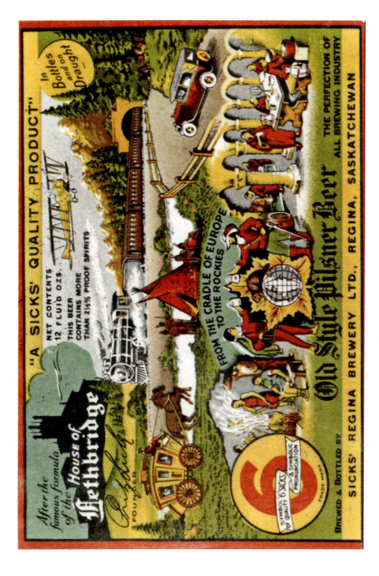

REMEMBER THIS NAME...

THE NEW BIG NAME IN BEER

"For top quality and flavor, give me BREWERS' BEST PREMIUM BEER every time," says Sammy Kaye, famous orchestra leader.

Yes, remember the name BREWERS' BEST whenever you want a great glass of beer. For everything about BREWERS' BEST spells quality... it's light, it's clean-tasting, and it's truly distinguished for its appetizing flavor and delicate bouquet.

BREWERS' BEST PREMIUM BEER marks the greatest advance in the brewing industry for over a century. It is brewed and bottled by a *country-wide group* of carefully selected prominent brewers whose combined experience and resources have produced this superior premium beer.

Remember the name — BREWERS' BEST PREMIUM BEER. And get set to enjoy the most distinctive beer you ever tasted... BREWERS' BEST, *the beer you've been waiting for!*

BREWERS' BEST *Premium* BEER
BREWERS' BEST ASSOCIATES, INC., 620 FIFTH AVE., NEW YORK

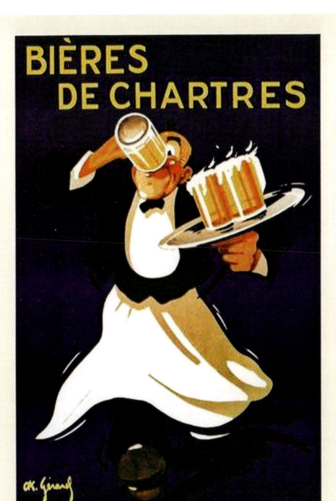

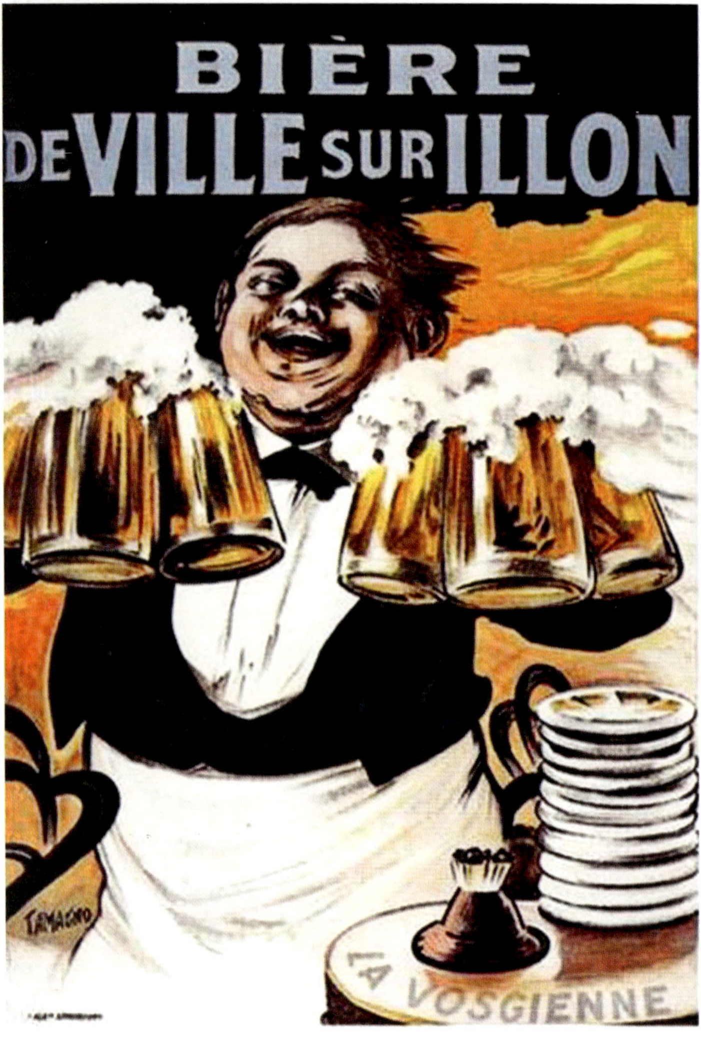
BIÈRE
DE VILLE SUR ILLON
LA VOSGIENNE

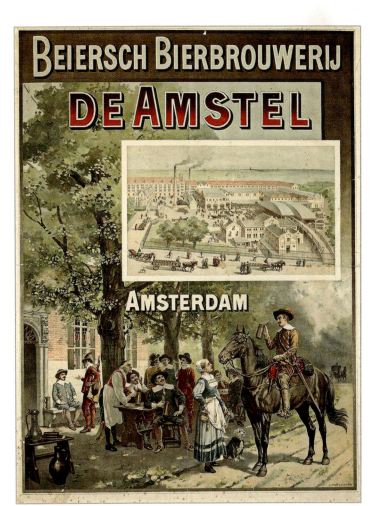

Pabst
The beer of quality
Bottled only at brewery in Milwaukee
Blue Ribbon

Retro Books

Unit 16 & 17. 12F, Tower A
New Mandarim Plaza,14
Science Museum Rd. TST East
Kowloon, Hong Kong

Printed in Chine